WHAT'S LEFT

WHAT'S LEFT

CONNIE K WALLE

MoonPath Press

Copyright © 2018 Connie K Walle

All rights reserved. No part of this publication may be reproduced, distributed, or transmitted in any form or by any means whatsoever without written permission from the publisher, except in the case of brief excerpts for critical reviews and articles. All inquiries should be addressed to MoonPath Press.

Poetry
ISBN 978-1-936657-39-1

Cover art: A Moment, acrylic on canvas, by painter Marie Fox

Visit Marie Fox online @
http://mariefoxpaintingaday.blogspot.com/

Author photo: by JCPenny Portraits

Design: Tonya Namura
using Gill Sans (display) and Gentium Book Basic (text)

MoonPath Press is dedicated to publishing the finest poets of the U.S. Pacific Northwest.

MoonPath Press
PO Box 445
Tillamook, OR 97141

MoonPathPress@gmail.com

http://MoonPathPress.com

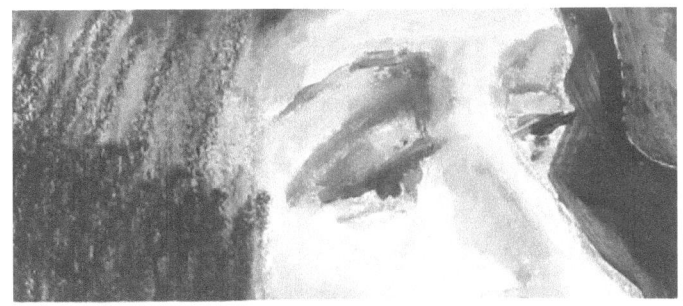

To the women of my critique group:
   Thank you for your tough love, your support.
   Without your encouragement this manuscript would
      not have happened.
   Thanks you to, Glenna Cook, Janet Frostad, Jo Forbes,
      and Diane Avery.

TABLE OF CONTENTS

1. SPINNING
Elsie at Fort Nisqually, 1847 ▪ 7
Sawdust ▪ 8
1948 Summer Night ▪ 9
Spinning ▪ 10
Not Everyone ▪ 12
Gym Class, 1952 ▪ 13
Freedom ▪ 15
Love Letters ▪ 16
We Never Talked ▪ 17
My Virginity Ached Like a Loose Tooth ▪ 18
Broken Teen ▪ 19
A Lady Doesn't Kiss and Tell ▪ 20
Long Distance Lover ▪ 21
Gardener, You've Dirt on Your Hands ▪ 22
Palm Reading ▪ 23

2. LOOKING FOR LOVE
Write Me A Love Poem ▪ 27
Of What's Left ▪ 28
Untimely ▪ 29
Burning Word Festival, Whidbey Island ▪ 30
Usted Hibrido ▪ 31
Looking for Love ▪ 32
Railroaded ▪ 33
Sadness ▪ 34
Closer ▪ 35
Under the Spotlight ▪ 36
She Wanted to Forgive Him ▪ 38
He Said   She Said ▪ 39
Pain as a Lover ▪ 40
But Will I Love You Tomorrow? ▪ 41
Boundaries ▪ 42
Treatise on Marriage ▪ 43

Alone ▪ 44
Desiccated ▪ 45
I Wouldn't Say My Sex Life Is Dead,
    But the Vultures are Circling ▪ 46
I Don't Have Hot Flashes, I Have Power Surges ▪ 47
A Word for Seasons ▪ 49

3. GOING THROUGH LIFE BACKWARDS
This Area Is Good for Wishes ▪ 53
What Voice ▪ 54
Trees Whisper Secrets ▪ 55
Talking to Saints ▪ 56
Death ▪ 57
Scrambled Broccoli ▪ 58
Summer Is Reluctant to Leave ▪ 59
For the Love of Sunday ▪ 60
Myth ▪ 61
My Fear ▪ 62
Still ▪ 63
Felled ▪ 64
Sacred Ground ▪ 65
A Look Is the Fire Itself ▪ 66
Fear ▪ 67
Memories ▪ 68
He Lies Dying ▪ 69
As the Sun ▪ 70
Mere Mortal ▪ 71
Dear Agnieszia ▪ 72
No One Home ▪ 73
An Inch ▪ 74
I'm Not Afraid of Death ▪ 75
Death's Kiss ▪ 76
Cancer Is a Four-Letter Word ▪ 77
What No One Told Me ▪ 78
Contemplating ▪ 79
Going Through Life Backwards ▪ 80

You Have to Let Go of the Solid Ground ▪ 81
Rule #1: Never use the word soul in a poem ▪ 82
The Silence of Death ▪ 83
Dying Wish ▪ 84

Acknowledgments ▪ 87
About the Author ▪ 89

WHAT'S LEFT

"But understanding a thing and accepting it are so very different things."

—Kat Zhang, *What's Left of Me*

I.
SPINNING

ELSIE AT FORT NISQUALLY, 1847

Dear Mama,
The mountains here are so beautiful.
Especially one they call Mt. Tacoma.

I owe my Mama a letter back at Boston.
I miss the soft leather shoes,
and petits fours at the parties.
How can I tell her about *here*
without making her worry?

The rain keeps fallin' in this desolate,
frightening country.
Lettuce barely grown,
corn not yet knee high
and it's August.
Peas and squash have blossomed
and died without producin'.

What will we do this winter—
live on potatoes which grow
anytime anyplace,
even in this unrelenting rain?

I don't have the money to buy flour
unless Henry sells the beaver pelts
at a better price than last year
and I'm pregnant with my third child.

Henry is a hard-workin', good man,
and treats me well.
He does love me.
That *should* be enough.

SAWDUST

While Mother and Daddy worked
at their restaurant,
I stayed home with Grandpa.

We were best molasses friends.
Grandpa was a carpenter.
My small hands helped to sand
the back of the violins he made.

He built the house where
I grew up after
we moved to Manitou.

It seems everything he did
or everywhere he went
smelled of sawdust
or fiddleback maple.

Today, my neighbors
are remodeling their apartment.
The odor of sawdust
infiltrates the steps,
the walls, the air.

I stop at the top of the stairs,
wish I could reach
for Grandpa's hand.
I lean into the wall,
take a deep breath,
hold his memory
in my lungs.

1948 SUMMER NIGHT

We laid on our backs in the grass,
pointed at the Big Dipper,
Orion's Belt,
made wishes on falling stars.

Before we set them free,
we caught fireflies in jars
we used as lanterns
when we played hide-and-seek.

Little did we know a time would come
when fireflies no longer existed,
city lights would outshine the stars,
and wishes were just a child's game.

SPINNING

I lie down for a nap,
hoping darkness will engulf me.
Instead, my mind spins
the events of today
with memories

that fly out the window,
through the barn,
picking up stray hay
and attaching to the horse harness
which hangs from a nail on the wall.

In the kitchen, recipes on 3x5 cards
shuffle themselves,
preparing to warm someone's tummy
or bring back a memory of
Francis' German Chocolate Cake.

Molecules emerge from the shadows,
thin specters of incompletion.
How can they be trusted
to stay in place
until planted on the paper?

They may sit for a while
at a table with a glass of rosé,
but can I keep their attention
long enough to lasso them
to settle in the ink?

I rise, slowly,
afraid the spinning
will knock me over,
that a wash of common sense
will erase everything.

NOT EVERYONE

Everyone has a spot where they feel comfortable and safe.

—Tom Adams

Not in my bedroom
where unwanted touch
found its way under sheets.

Not in the kitchen
where hands colored cheeks
and fingerprinted arms.

Not in the bathroom
where drowning
threatened every minute.

Not under the apple tree
in the backyard where
bark imprinted my back.

Not at school
where harsh words
cut deeper than knives.

Not in the haze
of colored bottles
and dirty needles.

Not even
in the quiet
of this cold grave.

GYM CLASS, 1952

Not today. No one-piece,
piss-yellow shorts gym suit.
Today we stay dressed
except for shoes.

Today is ballroom dance class.
I am thinking about the jacket
I designed to match the skirt
I will finish for my doll tonight.

I look up and Mrs. Brown
is staring down at me, saying,
"Miss Murray, didn't you hear me
call your name?"

I answer, "No Ma'am."
She grabs my arm
and pulls me out
to the middle of the gym floor.

"Pick a boy." she says.
I pick Robert, the hall monitor:
cute, dark hair, slender.
Doesn't really matter.

She practically drags Robert
onto the floor in front of me.
I smile, say "Don't worry."
(I know all the steps.)

My mother taught me to dance
before she taught me to walk.
Dancing with mother,
I never really connected it to boys.

I figured I would have to lead.
She takes his left hand
and places it in my right hand.
We hold it high, stand apart.

I put my hand on his shoulder.
He flinches. She places his right hand
on the small of my back.
Sweat beads up on his forehead.

We practice the box waltz, dancing
in a square. Like I said, I led.
Finally, the bell rings
and Robert runs to his next class.

I walk to my next class, realize
the small of my back is wet and warm
where his hand held me.
Wet and warm. Where he held me.

FREEDOM

Just a teenager more interested in boys
than news back then; no TV, cell phones, internet.

I didn't know there was war in the American streets;
battle to ride the front of the bus,
water fountain struggles.

At our house, there was music.
Jazz singers pounding black and white
keys into early dawn.

Heavy-set, ebony women, with gospel voices
hitting notes that shook the house.

Trumpets and slide trombones rocked our place,
having already put in hours at the bar.

They played for the feeling that
pushed through them,
like the high of cocaine and heroin.

I lay on the upstairs landing, flat on my stomach,
listening to freedom, unaware

of Malcom X, Martin Luther King Jr.,
the riots, the marches, the hate and the fear.

LOVE LETTERS

Hot-blooded Indian boy,
you wrote passionate letters
filled with scenes of love-making,
which in my naiveté, I did not grasp,

but Mama did
when she found your letters
tucked away in my dresser,
with the prison return address.

Forbidden to write to you again,
even to explain why I had to stop.
Your memory hung over my shoulder
like a shadow.

Full-moon face, olive skin, shiny
black hair slicked back, muscles bulging
under your white t-shirt—
"Eat your heart out Marlon Brando."

I've since forgotten the church retreat
where we met and exchanged addresses,
but your flashing eyes and warm smile
remain with the letters bundled and tied
in the bottom of my cedar chest.

WE NEVER TALKED
for my mother

You thought I would stay sixteen,
forever virginal to the outside world.

I knew you would be fighting dragons,
didn't realize you could be lured
by the maidens they captured.

Left alone, I explored the darkness
of the caves and cliffs within,
growing stronger with each descent.

You never noticed that the more
dragons you slew,
the more they multiplied.

One day, I stepped outside the door,
found a world full of colors, sounds, faces.

You took the same path home each night.
Your form relaxed into the shape of the chair,
while I was dancing in the street.

MY VIRGINITY ACHED LIKE A LOOSE TOOTH
—*Joanne Henry Allred,* particles

I could have been one of *those* girls.
In high school, they were called easy.

By graduation, they had left school
to visit aunts in Minnesota.

With my luck, I kept dating boys
who wanted to protect my virginity.

My hands wandered into places
they didn't belong, my wrists were

grabbed, my hands placed in the folds
of the skirt, where they did belong.

So, when a man came along and paid me
attention—well, *that* kind of attention,

I married him. Then I found out he had
this attitude that nice girls didn't do *those things.*

Yes, I did it, more than the three children
I bore him, but it wasn't hot, fun, tempestuous.

It was never like in the movies, and
I still yearn for the backseat of a Mustang.

BROKEN TEEN

Like a robot with its nodes
solidly welded, his nerves do not
respond to the environment.
No matter what he does,
no one responds to him.
He is never enough.

He lasers in on what others
feel, but cannot feel it
for himself. It is his fault
his mother is unhappy, his dad
doesn't call, he has no friends.

His barometer can't find its
mean value, so he is swamped
with confusion. If he is kind,
it is interpreted as passive.
When he is strong, then rude.

He turns to alcohol, but
even that doesn't work.
Now he must find another way.
A way to find peace.
He waits for dark
to walk the bridge into town.

A LADY DOESN'T KISS AND TELL

How many others? he asks,
as he nibbles my ear.

I don't remember, I reply,
*except those who left
scars on my heart.*

*But tell me, am I
the 4th or 17th or 29th?*

I laugh and say, *Never mind,
just kiss me here, here, and here*,
as I point to cheek,
neck, and shoulder.

He kisses where I point
His hands find all the right places.

You, I sigh, *you are the first
not yet to break my heart.*

LONG DISTANCE LOVER

You come to me from Denver,
Chicago, or Tallahassee.
You strip off your jeans
as though it were
only yesterday I saw you last.

In the meld of skin,
sweat, and kisses, I forget
the wind calls your name
like a red-headed lover.

The next time we meet,
it will have been Peoria,
Houston, or Albuquerque.

GARDENER, YOU'VE DIRT ON YOUR HANDS

You tell me
I am pretty
as a rose.

That the softness
of my petals
makes up for
the occasional
sharp thorns.

I keep finding myself
in this vase alone,
my petals dropping
one by one,
my leaves curling.

Rumor has it—
you've been seen
out in the garden
among the daisies.

PALM READING

The palm holds a line
strong with the desire toward learning.

The lifeline struggles to begin,
then becomes wider, deeper,
seems to extend forever.

The heart line is steady and loyal.

Lots of smaller lines
indicate a sensitivity not usually
shown to strangers, such as
fingers which yearn to caress your face,
a thumb wanting to stroke your wet, soft lips.

The palm is open to new experiences.

Yet, there is no indication of the hard work
this hand has performed in the call to duty.

No fingers stained with the ink of a writer.
Not a trace of moisture left from tears.

2. LOOKING FOR LOVE

WRITE ME A LOVE POEM

Fill it with my favorite
flower and perfume,
a glass of champagne,
a bite of caviar.

Whisper *sweet words* to me,
your back turned
to the other people
in the room.

Let your face light up
with delight,
thoughts close to your heart,
you will share later
at a better time and place.

After 30 years,
there can still be surprises.
This is your chance
and I am waiting.

OF WHAT'S LEFT

Maybe I've been reading
too many romance books
or looking in the mirror
overly often,
seeing the ruins
as my body crumbles
like a Mayan Temple.

In my dreams,
I remember his touch,
and times we danced
the night away.
How he softly
spoke my name,
as our bodies
discovered each other.

I wonder what changed.
When did he stop loving me?
When did I no longer
care if he did?
Was our love
ever strong
enough to last?

I check the obituaries,
scan for his name,
but they don't tell me
if he thinks of me or
has any regrets.

UNTIMELY

My time melts
                away
My dreams, like wax
drip into the
                past
I have to wonder
which life is
                this
How many times
will I make the same
                mistakes
Where is the passion
I thought we all were
entitled to
Why do words
ink and paper
haunt my every minute
                steal
my soul away
leave me tired
as a candle's
                last breath

BURNING WORD FESTIVAL, WHIDBEY ISLAND

I fell in love like a man who finds
a '57 Chevy like he had in high school.

I fell in love with words, with the lips that spread
those words over my body like kisses.

My skin tingly, my heart raced. I fell in love/hate
with young people who write better than I ever will.

I fell in love with women who found their voices,
told their stories of baking, ironing, and sex.

I fell in love with cheese which was as tasty as poetry,
and with poetry which was as tasty as cheese.

I fell in love with laughter that rang from the rafters,
followed by cries of "Encore! Encore!"

I fell in love with tears and silence that followed
poems against war and loss and left us

holding our breaths in our palms.

USTED HIBRIDO
(You Bastard)

After muddy boots
cross my floor,
sweaty shirts,
childbirth,
scrimping pesos to buy
masa for tortillas,
making the beans
last one more day,
you finally get a better job.

The children are older,
we have time for ourselves.
My waist is a little wider.
My breasts hang limp.
You decide you want that
child of a woman next door.
You grind this diamond
under your heel to dust
good only for a nail file.

LOOKING FOR LOVE

I hear the rumble
from deep within,
feel the shift of
tectonic plates.
Try to balance myself.
Hear the echo from
that hole we try
all our lives to fill.
Realize I've failed again,
as you slam the front door.

RAILROADED

I am going north
and you are headed south.

There's a clack-clack of words
without communication—
no agreement or disagreement.

Unable to bridge the gap
or pull into the station.

You, high speed,
not willing to slow.

Me, constant, strong, on time.
Doesn't matter—rain or shine,
there will never be an arrival.

SADNESS

You are the vulture, picking
my bones clean of memories.

I don't have time for you.
I must keep moving, find food

for my children, quiet in a temple,
hold them to my breast

away from terror. Do not flash pictures
of my brothers playing hide-and-seek,

for they will never see brides,
nor children of their own.

Find someone else to torment.
Remove that mirror full of tears.

I must bury you here
with the other unmarked graves.

I have work to do, a journey to complete.
Where it will take me, I don't know.

CLOSER

It isn't remembering my alcoholic
father, paranoid mother,
verbally abusive boss.

It is the words I should have said
when my daughter
needed me most.

It isn't losing my hearing, sight, or
ability to walk without falling.
It isn't the trip to England I didn't take.

It is the mother who never saw
who I was
because I didn't know who I was.

It isn't the job at the University
I didn't get, or the one I left undone.
It isn't having *not* learned to ski.

It is the time sharp words spit from
my tongue
when I should have been kinder.

Isn't not loving you. It
is
not telling you.

UNDER THE SPOTLIGHT

I hear him as I go by.

He says it again,
the name of someone he loves.

His lips keep moving,
whisper sounds
like twin poplars in wind.

The bench he sits on
under the light
is weathered, dry and brittle,
like him.

People pass,
stare and wonder,
women with babies in pushcarts,
small boys on bikes red as cherries.

Still he sits.

Now, from the café,
I watch him carefully,
wonder which breath
will be his last.

A light sprinkle of rain starts.
He doesn't seem to notice.

Then, more rain.

Now water runs down
the foggy window.

He continues his conversation
with himself.

The street has cleared.
No one pays him any mind.

I watch with morbid fascination—
wonder if I, too, will die in Paris,
alone, on a rainy day.

SHE WANTED TO FORGIVE HIM

There could have been forgiveness if he had used
her name instead of calling her Jeannie during a fight
over something so small, almost invisible.

Her breath stopped, her eyes went gray,
like she would faint.
He didn't realize what he had said,
until he looked at her.
She had come undone, feral like an injured coyote.

The name slid onto the floor, crawled across the room,
trying to disappear or behave like it didn't exist,
seeking a place to hide,
a way to make itself into something else.

She curled into a ball, her sobs so loud, the neighbors
called the police. They thought he was killing her,
stabbing her in the heart over and over.

He tried to explain, or make it go away, but it grew
like yeast bread in a bowl. No matter what he said,
it got bigger and bigger until he left the house,
drove away.

Her pain is the broken vase that once held
good memories,
or it sits on her shoulder like a stock,
constant rubbing of metal against skin.
No end, no end to the pain at all.

HE SAID	**SHE SAID**

HE SAID

Moonlight caressed
her breast
while I watched her lips,
wet with my kisses,
whisper my name
    as in a prayer.

SHE SAID

Fogged over
windows
bend the moonlight
that moments before
reflected off the sweat
    of your back.

PAIN AS A LOVER

He begins by caressing my back,
then his hand slides past my waist and hip.
He nibbles the back of my knee.

Then, wanting to play rougher,
the bite to my calf is sharp and deep.
He rakes his fingers through my hair
until my head aches, forcing my eyes open
out of a deep sleep I can't return to.

He comes to me more and more,
and someday, he will hold me tightly
until my eyes close and my breath stops.

BUT WILL I LOVE YOU TOMORROW?

I know you love me, your favorite
shirt is the button-down blue one
with the almost invisible pinstripe.

I know you love *The New York Times*,
leave it on the coffee table after reading
to save the crossword puzzle.

I know you could walk a million miles in
your tennis shoes and would trade them
for your penny loafers any day.

I know you remember my birthday,
the day we got engaged, our first date,
the day Mama died, my favorite flowers.

I know you wear a suit and tie to work, but
if the business was yours, every day would
be casual Friday with sleeves rolled-up, no tie.

I know the time is coming quickly when I will
no longer recognize you, ask *Who are you*
and *what are you doing in my house*
and *why have you brought me daffodils?*

BOUNDARIES

Not just lines
on maps,
nor rules
in a book.
Feelings trapped,
anger like plate glass
in front of me.
Work too hard
for my body,
wages too small
to feed our children.
Loneliness
wrapped like a blanket
as I sit in the dark.

TREATISE ON MARRIAGE

For fifty years she
subjugated herself for him.

Placated her soul with violin
lessons and poetry workshops.

Then when she should be warm and
comfortable with grandchildren at her feet,

he moved her to a cold, hard state,
away from friends and family.

I weep for her.

Or, do I weep for myself, who is afraid
to give all for love?

ALONE

Alone defines a life.
Loneliness goes clear to the bone.
Lonely, even as a wife
in a house that's not a home.

Loneliness goes clear to the bone.
Breath presses against my spine
in a house that's not a home,
nothing like a shrine.

Breath presses against my spine.
Nothing helps—not drugs, nor tears.
Nowhere is there a shrine.
This loneliness will hang on for years.

Nothing helps—not drugs, nor tears.
This curse has come my stay.
This loneliness will hang on for years.
There is nothing more to say.

This curse has come to stay—
lonely, even as a wife.
There is nothing more to say.
Alone defines a life.

DESICCATED

> *My sex life is so desiccated I'm going to paint*
> *a sign on my front door that reads* Men.
> —attributed to Dorothy Parker

Dry as sand dunes in Oregon
Windless as wheat fields in Wenatchee
Brittle as underbrush in the Olympic Forest

You know what danger that leads to...

everything
                everything
                                will burst into flame

I WOULDN'T SAY MY SEX LIFE IS DEAD, BUT THE VULTURES ARE CIRCLING
—Maxine, *The Queen of Crabbiness*

Depression slides into my pocket as easy as a dime.
I remember a love-life once upon a time.

Warm hands finding places I never knew I owned.
Pushing buttons then discovered, now long left alone.

A head upon a pillow, one that wasn't mine.
Soft words spoken sweetly, his love for me defined.

Oh, sweet were his kisses, as moonlight crossed the bed.
Touches gentle and loving, though not a word was said.

Many years have come and gone,
my hair long has been gray.

The memories of those special nights
have never gone away.

I DON'T HAVE HOT FLASHES, I HAVE POWER SURGES

Oh dear! Here comes a hot flash.
I feel it barreling through.
Hits me like a freight train.
I don't know what to do.

I try to think real positive.
I say, "this too shall pass,"
as I white-knuckle grip the desk,
my eyes glaze over like glass.

I blush from head to toe,
the flush runs unrestrained.
I try to say, "it's youthful glow,"
but the hot flash is to blame.

I see visions overhead
flashing off and on—
of empty nest and sagging breasts,
then, in seconds they are gone.

Now, I know these years
it is said, really are the best.
The kids are gone and
God knows, I need the rest.

My life is just beginning,
though the media says it's done,
that youth and beauty is the thing
and I'm no longer young.

Well, I've got news for you kid.
I'm really at my peak.
If I can just survive these hot flashes
and live another week.

A WORD FOR SEASONS

Once more we pass from the sweat of summer
to the cleansing rains of fall.
Again, the reds, rusts, and golds steal our breath,
rob the plum, apple, and cherry of their gifts.

I love to walk through the park,
watch the colors vie for attention,
wave good-bye to the Canadian geese.

I watch unknown people
stand beside the lake talking,
not knowing the lake hears their secrets.

I know the lake listens to their lies,
sees past the shadows of their indiscretions,
leaves them to toss and turn in their sleep,
knows they plot against love.

3.
GOING THROUGH LIFE BACKWARDS

THIS AREA IS GOOD FOR WISHES

The towns are named
after corporations, Indians, and women:
Carnation, Colville, Marysville.

A large bolder lies in the middle of the river,
a white stripe all the way around,
but too big for wishes.

Clouds, like popcorn, dot the mountains.
Garage sales line the roadside
now that the hay has been baled.

Smoke can be seen in the distance.
A wildfire from lightning or a warning
that winter is hiding behind that hill.

WHAT VOICE

Chief Leschi Daffodil Princess Dies of Apparent Suicide.
—newspaper headline 4/11/2012

Did Mother Earth whisper
in her ear, *Turn into dust?*

Did Father Sky invite her to join
the Ancestor Pow Wow?

Did the Salmon call her
to follow upstream?

Did Raven trick her into fading
into the dark with him?

Did a voice so dark and cold
frighten her to follow its directions?

Did a weeping voice
softly call her name?

TREES WHISPER SECRETS

Shell peas into a wooden bowl
while sitting on the front porch.

Peel the homegrown tomatoes
and slip into mason jars.

Watch the pressure cooker steam and whistle.

Chop the dill and measure the pickle brine.
Dice the onions.

Unpack the quilt your mother made
from your childhood dresses.

Buy new shoes with sturdy soles,
and rain boots.

Check the fir trees one more time,
and count the cones.

TALKING TO SAINTS

Do I stand, sit or lay prone
with my arms and legs spread
as on a cross,
my face pressed into the carpet.

I chose to sit.
My hands rest on the chair's arms,
palms up.
My eyes closed.

Who do I call?
St. Christopher,
Goddess of healing Gula
or Quan Yen?
Will they fight over
who gets to answer?

Do I say hello,
Dear Sir or Madame?
Please or Mon Dieu!

This talking to saints
is an exhausting matter,
but you take the needed steps
to ask for your brother's life.

DEATH

Confusion covers everyone
like a quilt,
but not comforting.

Tears dry as plans are made,
remade,
unmade.

Family is called,
memories are unpacked,
packed away.

Furniture is arranged
to accommodate guests.
Folding chairs set up.

Food cooked by neighbors
comes wrapped
in yesterday's newspaper.

I still feel your hand in mine,
warm
and slowly turning colder.

SCRAMBLED BROCCOLI

Seven-thirty, Tuesday
    becomes
        eleven pounds, three days.

My granddaughter Annabelle
    becomes
        Belladonna.

Though I'm not sure that wasn't
    a Freudian slip.

My street Grandview
    becomes
        Golf Bay Walk.

Should I be afraid of Dementia
or is this just another poem about sex?

SUMMER IS RELUCTANT TO LEAVE

She wraps her warm breath
around me as I lie naked
on the sheets.
I am not her lover.

I wait for Fall.
He is on the way.
Trees already
prepare for his arrival.

They dress in their best
red dresses
and gold jewelry.
People will not recognize him.

They will call him *Indian Summer.*
I will know him
when his morning kiss
is cool and wet with dew.

FOR THE LOVE OF SUNDAY

Covered with a blanket of poetry books,
I nap this Sunday afternoon,
having read until I was depleted.
What if I died like this?
Barnstone in my lap,
Lux on my breast,
Finney pressed against my hip.
Would my children guess
by the smile on my lips,
I died from an orgasm of words?

MYTH

This Cinderella withers
on the hearth,
no longer in full bloom,

but dry and brittle,
pressed between the pages
of time.

Even if
Prince Charming
did come charging up

on his white steed
he would be too damn old
to get off the horse.

Other princes ride past
to Sleeping Beauty's castle
to awaken her from ageless slumber.

Excuse me,
but I have to take these ashes
out back to the rose garden.

MY FEAR

Not the smell of burning ash,
nor a cold dark grave,
but a chilling mist
that steals words, names,
end of sentences, memories.

A younger woman who stands
in front of me, holds tight
her smile, eyes filled with water,
as I ask, "Who are you?
Why are you here?"

STILL

A newborn, home, sleeping.
Trees wait for the wind to stroke their leaves.
Water lily on small pond in the park.
Watching the sun move to the horizon.
The nude statue of David in the Louvre.

After fifty years of marriage, his touch.
The moon closer to the earth than before.
The Ferris wheel at the top of the turn.
Tears poised to drop as a favorite song plays.
Your breath when the brakes give way.

FELLED

Broken as a fallen oak,
he sits on the bucket;
yesterday's newspaper
protecting the bones of his butt.

As I bend to place a dollar in
the Tully's Coffee cup,
he partially raises his head
as if to say thank you.

I stare into his eyes
and there is no one there.
There hasn't been anyone
for some time.

Don't we need love, or passion
or desire to keep us alive?
When did he leave this body?
How does it keep going without him?

There must be some sort of life
as birds don't land on him,
though his bony shoulder
would make a good perch.

What kind of monument
is this downed oak of a man?
Like an abandoned gravesite,
he sits, day after day, in the rain.

SACRED GROUND

I won't eat oysters.
I hate seagulls, also
sand between my toes.

I am a native here,
so you would think
I would write about
sand and sea and shells.

This place is mountains
and trees so green
they hurt the eyes.

The quiet is so deep
you can feel the velvet
touch of the wind.

There are rocks that
fit your hand just right
and hold the perfect color
of sanctity.

I watch the colorless stream
roll over boulders,
know that salmon
worship here too.

A LOOK IS THE FIRE ITSELF

Smoke fills the living room,
the couch, the chair,
only charred shadows.

She stands in the center,
seeing it all.

Fire licks the tips of her shoes,
jumps to her skirt.

She raises her arms
above her head.

Fire climbs her arms,
leaps to her hair.

When the fire department arrives,
they find only ashes, and ghosts
fleeing through the backyard.

FEAR

In her own house,
she wandered from room to room,
counted knickknacks and old pictures.

Lived like a well-read novel.

Now she lives in a care center
where breakfast is served
on their clock, not hers.

She doesn't recognize her room
when she returns.

She keeps looking for things
she used to have,
then forgets what they were.

Sounds, names, and places
disappear like an early morning cloud.

She keeps looking into the dark,
hoping she will recognize anything.
Panic raises hair on her arms.

She repeats my name over and over.

MEMORIES

I dissect her life piece by piece:
needle point, crochet,
embroidery, tatting, knitting.

Sweaters for granddaughters,
tea cups for nieces,
boxes and boxes of birthday cards
received and saved.

Bibles next to books
on how to be psychic.

Dishes saved
because they were Emilie's,
although they were broken
and re-glued.

A friend, helping me sort through, said,
*She sure was well rounded
in thought and actions.*
How could he see this in all her belongings?

I knew it because I lived with her,
babysat her boys.
She cared for me when I was ill.
Prayed on Sundays,
read cards or psalms, other times.

She was my "other mother"
when my mother worked.
She was my friend
when my friends were gone.

HE LIES DYING

All he ever knew were engines—
what made them purr
when he talked to them.

His lips rarely moved with
Wow, what a great dinner
or *that was a wonderful party.*

He never knew those *three little words.*

Never whispered them
to find out how
they could have changed his life.

His son stands at the edge of the bed.
Holds out his hand,
hopes for one little crumb.

AS THE SUN

is shoved
into the sea
by the lateness
of the day,
am I the only one
who notices
the bruised clouds
on the horizon
and the tears
that fall
in the distance?

MERE MORTAL

I burn the incense.
Light the candles.
Chant to the four
directions.

I mix the herbs and
repeat the blessings.
I thank the Goddess
for her goodness and love.

No magic, no power,
no telepathy.
I cannot put Humpty Dumpty
together again.
Nor can I stop missing you.

DEAR AGNIESZIA

Before you were nine
all things should have
been spoken.
The lines tossed to you
light as jacks, and just
as sharp, bouncing
round your head, dribbling
into your ear.
But you know
I loved you and that
should count for something.

NO ONE HOME

For the soule the bodie forme doth take;
For soul is forme and doth the bodie make.
   —Edmund Spenser

The windows, the dark
of an empty house.
No warm glow, no welcome
at the door.

Voices crying "help me, help me"
echo through the halls.
The rocker moves back
and forth, back and forth.

I knew she'd leave me someday.
What I didn't know is that
she would vacate without notice
and leave this shell behind.

AN INCH

Death takes a lot out of you,
even when it is not your own.
The arrangements, the calls,
the sorting through memories.

Like water on a rock
you eventually wear thin.
*You're an inch shorter since
your mother died,* the Doctor said.

I'm not surprised.
Somehow I knew
when she left,
she took a piece of me.

I'M NOT AFRAID OF DEATH

I'm afraid of the dark as I find
my way around bones and rocks,
choosing the wrong door,
finding fire and brimstone,
instead of a lifetime of living in Paris.

I'm afraid of screaming
and no one will hear me.
I'm afraid when I find the moon,
it will be sharp enough to cut my throat.

DEATH'S KISS

Death is a handsome young man
with dark shiny, slicked-back hair,
sea green eyes you can drown in,
a soft seductive voice.

It is Old Age I am afraid of.
He is an ugly, hungry old man,
long white hair,
bony fingers with beauty-shop nails.

He says he just wants to nibble a little.
First, he nibbles a little memory:
I forget time, phone numbers,
grandchildren's names, and dates.

When he chews on my ear,
I find myself saying, "What? What?"
He bites deep into the muscles.
I walk a little slower.

He craves the liver and kidneys,
but you don't want to hear the results of that.
One day, I will find myself in a strange room
with strange people who wipe my nose and butt.

I will comb my hair, smudge on some lipstick,
dress in my very best nightgown,
lie down on my bed and whisper
Please come, sweet death, come kiss me.

CANCER IS A FOUR-LETTER WORD

No axe to a healthy tree, but a fungus
silently moves up the roots
to a soft spot here or there.

It slices a mother's first connection
to her child, threatens a man's sexuality.
Friends whisper to friends.

Sufferers don't know if they should "tell all"
and be thought complaining.
Friends are afraid to say *the word* out loud.

Survivors know it can go either way.
Those of us unknowing, hold their hands,
drive to doctor appointments, silently pray.

Suspended on this tight rope,
stretched over a dubious net,
our loved ones' worlds spin out of control.

We hand them the best umbrella we have
and hope it will be enough
to maintain their balance.

WHAT NO ONE TOLD ME

You lose your favorite food,
your knees, your hearing and sight,
to be replaced with pain or pills.

Then you lose your friends one by one.
Finally your best friend leaves
in her own personalized box.

This isn't just a punch in the gut.
This is your insides being pulled out
and slung on the ground.

This was the woman who
went through everything with you:
your promotion,
your firstborn's wedding,
when that bastard left you
with a broken heart.

This was the woman who insisted
you go dancing when you wanted
to stay home and sulk,
fed you when funds were short.

This was the woman you could call
at 3:00 a.m. and know
she would listen to you.

Now, she is gone.
You pick up the phone to call,
then place it back into the cradle.
Sit down and cry.

CONTEMPLATING

A friend leaves. We run out of ice cream. Harsh words cut a little of our heart away. We outgrow a favorite pair of jeans. Each day is a day of contemplation. The daffodil's bloom drops back to soil. We get fired from our job or find a new job we hate. Falling out of love or love falling away from us. Wills are written, doctors are notified of our wishes, but the day and date can't be set. We can only try to say *good-bye* and *I love you* before *I'm sorry I didn't tell them.*

GOING THROUGH LIFE BACKWARDS

I lag behind progress or development,
turned in the opposite direction,
life arranged in the wrong order,
unsure of myself,
reluctant to move forward.

I shake it off, try something new,
but it clings like snot.
Will this curse follow me always?

I approach with caution,
hesitant to protest,
when all others are
fighting conventions,
at odds with myself
for no good reason.

One step at a time,
class after class,
I hope for some magical change.
I do not understand why
I remain the way I am.

Then, one day, I find the answer
from a strange source—
a voice asking,
Were you born breach?
butt forward, head last,
mother screaming?

YOU HAVE TO LET GO OF THE SOLID GROUND
(title by Libby Wagner)

Pen in hand,
doesn't write itself.

Wadding across the page
stringing words doesn't
bring relief, nor inspiration.

OK, the fear is there,
beside the desire for greatness.

Fear is just a word
which neither helps
nor creates greatness.

You stare at the page,
dream of accolades
and dried link.

The pen waivers,
cleaves to the page,
but seems to have
no ink to spare
when you need it most.

You wave your magic wand,
call to your muse,
and pray she answers.

RULE #1: NEVER USE THE WORD SOUL IN A POEM

That place
where life begins—
      it can be defamed.

Where love, fear,
and anguish abound—
      it can be cursed.

A place tears gather
in joy and sorrow—
      it can be bruised or burnt.

A precious space
only yours to fill or empty—
      it can be misled.

One thing no one can
take from you—
      it stays pure.

THE SILENCE OF DEATH
with a quote from *Pale Horse, Pale Rider*
by Katherine Anne Porter

"Daylight strikes with a sudden blow"
as to awaken me.

How I have loved this house
where I am woven together
like a spider web.

I have wept here,
laughed here,
been too angry,
and too outrageous.

Yet this shell is all I have of me.
Now silenced,
I have no speech,
I am deaf.
I am separate from all living things.

I am
but memory.

DYING WISH

Box me not in satin and pine,
but gift me of fir and flowers,
or sea and shells, or
                a little of both.

Mix a little sand and sage
with my bones.
Let the wind call my name
                for the last time.

Don't dampen the soil with tears,
but let a wish or a prayer
be consumed in the flames
                of my passing.

Rejoice with my spirit,
and if you need me,
call to me in your dreams.

Then, watch billboards
                for my answer.

ACKNOWLEDGMENTS

My thanks to the following periodicals, in which some of the poems in this volume first appeared, sometimes in earlier versions:

Apricorn: "Under the Spotlight"

Avalon Literary Review: "Of What's Left"

Kindofahurricane: "A Look Is the Fire Itself"

Motherhood: "An Inch"

Perspective: "Fear"

Poetry Atlas: "Elsie at Ft. Nisqually, 1947," "This Area Is Good for Wishes"

Pontoon: "Alone"

Protest Poems: "Should I Apologize"

Puyallup Gallery: "We Never Talked"

Quiet Courage: "Boundaries"

Quill and Parchment: "1948 Summer," "A Word For Seasons," "Gardener, You've Dirt on Your Hands," "Summer Is Reluctant to Leave"

Raven Chronicles: "Dying Wish"

Sarasvati Takes Pegasus as Her Mount: "Mere Mortal"

Senior Scene: "What Voice?"

Suisun Valley Review: "Sacred Ground"

Survival Chronicles: "Sadness"

Tacoma Writers Anthology: "I'm Not Afraid of Death"

Tahoma's Shadow: "Cancer is a Four-Letter Word"

Womankind: "Myth"

ABOUT THE AUTHOR

Connie K Walle is a life-long Pacific Northwest resident of Tacoma, Washington, and is President and Founder of Puget Sound Poetry Connection where she hosts the "Distinguished Writer Series," now in its 27th year.

Connie also founded *Our Own Words,* a teen writing contest in conjunction with Pierce Library. It is now in its 21st year.

Her awards include: The 2015 Amocat Award for promotion of the arts, Margaret K Williams Award in support of the arts, Washington Poets Association Faith Beamer Cooke Award, Metro Parks Certificate of Appreciation, and City of Tacoma Certificate of Appreciation for community service.

Connie has three children and nine grown grandchildren.

www.ingramcontent.com/pod-product-compliance
Lightning Source LLC
Chambersburg PA
CBHW021445080526
44588CB00009B/696